THE THINKER'S POCKETBOOK

By Angelena Boden

Drawings by Phil Hailstone

D0711482

"Clarifies why some thinking processes are more effective than others and explains how the use of different thinking skills can help ensure efficient decision-making."
Marion Nixon, Tourism Manager, Derby City Council

"Gives you that immediate, unexpected nudge to see things differently - to allow your brain to take off in a direction that can prove invaluable in seeing a 'problem' from a different angle, thereby coming closer to resolving it."
Geoff Pine, Principal, Woolwich College

Dedication: to my husband Hamid and my daughters Anousheh and Anisa who occupy many of my thoughts.

CONTENTS

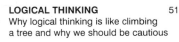

INTRODUCTION

THINKING: WHY & WHAT?

It is estimated that we have over 50,000 thoughts a day - positive, negative, frightening, enlightening or just crazy thoughts. They can be triggered by:

- Flashbacks (memory) and visual images
- Words, snippets of conversation (even from childhood)
- Familiar and unfamiliar objects, scenes, patterns, problems, tasks and people
- Emotions - curiosity, anxiety, regret, anger, sadness
- And simply doing nothing

Sometimes we engineer thoughts or they simply leap into our minds unexpectedly. We accept, question, challenge or discard them. Some tumble around in confusion, become exaggerated and irrational, causing anxiety and mental paralysis.

Thinking is healthy. We need to think to understand, to learn and to progress, and to collect and assimilate information before deciding what to do with it. But, the thinking process needs to be managed and channelled constructively.

ARE WE TAUGHT TO THINK?

This is a **BIG** question.

We copy patterns of behaviour and absorb ideas from those who influenced us in childhood. These thinking processes are assumed to be the right and only ones - until challenged by someone else.

We can become entrenched in a mind-set which is later difficult to unlearn. Mind-sets inhibit the thinking process, can lead to bias, stubbornness and prejudice:

'He has a closed mind.'

'I have a mental block with this.'

'You're so set in your ways.'

'Tried and tested methods are the best.'

These statements reflect just how fixed some people are in their thinking. Such people look for justification of their ideas which, in turn, reinforces the mind-set - an ever decreasing circle.

THINKING & ATTITUDES

How we think affects our attitude to life:

- The **positive thinker** becomes successful because he believes he will be

- The **creative thinker** knows there is a solution to a problem, however impossible it seems

- The **bottom-line thinker** will take calculated risks because she has evaluated the 'worst possible scenario' and has accepted it

- For the **negative thinker**, however, life is fraught, unproductive, complicated and something to be survived rather than enjoyed

SELF-PERCEPTION

How we think depends on how we see ourselves.

Would you describe yourself as any of the following:

- Powerful
- Interesting
- Creative
- A follower
- Easily discouraged

- Trapped
- Always to blame
- Charming/witty
- Untalented
- Special

Ask yourself why? Where have these images about yourself come from?

Do they affect your thinking?

EXERCISES

To fully benefit, begin by exercising your mind. Ideas and thoughts are fixed by:

Doing   Exercise: Try tying your shoelaces, scarf, tie or knot differently from your usual way.

Visualising   Exercise: Superimpose a map of England on India and consider the differences in population density. What does that tell you about the potential for doing business in India?

Discussing   Exercise: Play devil's advocate in a meeting. Get into the boss's shoes when being grilled. Practise empathy.

Realising that anything is possible, if you think it's possible, prepares you for The Thinker's Pocketbook.

POSITIVE THINKING

POSITIVE THINKING

BELIEF SYSTEM IMPACT

Positive thinkers will have been influenced by the belief system they have developed from childhood. Listening to parents, relatives, teachers and adults in the outside world, children might develop a negative or positive belief system which affects their thought processes.

Negative belief system

- Men are not to be trusted
- After 40 it's downhill all the way
- There's bound to be a catch; it's too good to be true

Positive belief system

- We always have choices
- There's always a solution
- Tomorrow is another day

NEGATIVE THINKERS

- Make excuses for not doing/completing tasks
- Lay blame when things go wrong
- Give up too easily
- Tend to see the negative in everything
- Devalue others and themselves
- Believe they can't before they have tried
- Moan, complain, criticise
- Feel angry, resentful, envious

9

POSITIVE THINKERS

- See problems as challenges
- Live fully in the here and now
- Keep an open mind; all ideas and suggestions are possible
- Push out negative thoughts as they enter the mind
- Add up what they have rather than what they don't have
- Don't listen to tales of woe from others
- Don't make excuses but take action

SPOTTING POSITIVE THINKERS

- They use positive language:
  'Yes, I'll have a go; something will
  work out; she's good natured'
- They use positive gestures:
  smile, walk tall, use expressive
  hand gestures, nod
- They use a lively, enthusiastic,
  friendly tone of voice
- They care about how they present
  themselves to the outside world

(11)

GOOD & BAD VIEWPOINTS

Positive thinking requires you to take the view that there is a bright and a dark side to everything. Positive thinkers see something good and something bad in anything and everyone. They acknowledge this then decide to **select** positive thoughts.

Exercise

1. Select a plain drinking glass and put it on the table in front of you.
2. Think negatively for a moment and describe the glass. You might say it is: plain, boring, colourless, cheap, common or vulgar.
3. Now look at it again, but think positively about it. Simple, inexpensive, popular or easy to replace might come to mind.

You have the **choice**.

POSITIVE THINKING

VISUALISE TO REALISE

Positive thinkers **visualise** then **realise**.

Unlike the unrealistically ambitious, positive thinkers take a few small but manageable steps to convert a simple idea into a practical achievement.

Success in small measures results in confidence, further vision, bigger ideas - greater achievements lead to more positive thinking.

Visualise yourself as an artist, in a new home, driving the car of your choice, taking your trip of a lifetime. Keep it in the forefront of your mind; have a picture of it on your desk, fridge, dashboard but don't lose sight of it.

Take it slowly - have a realistic action plan - and focus on what you have achieved not what remains to be achieved.

POSITIVE THINKING

BEING POSITIVE AT WORK

1. Ask yourself a few questions:
- Do I have the skills, qualifications?
- Do I have the will-power?
- Is this what I want or what I feel I should have?
- Why do I want this?

2. Devise an action plan. Positive thinkers don't try to do too much at once.

Example

A positive thinker wishing to gain better qualifications to achieve promotion, will:
- Check out courses, qualifications, colleges
- Decide how much time is needed
- Analyse realistically how much time can be spared
- Explore possibilities for time off work or work-based study
- Make a weekly plan to build in the time
- Begin with stage one and complete this successfully before moving on

POSITIVE THINKING

DEVELOP A POSITIVE THEME FOR THE DAY

Positive thinking is encouraged by devising a formula, a mantra which begins with **'I will'**. Example:

- **I will** view positively everything today throws at me and not think about tomorrow

- **I will** try to see some good in people and in every situation, no matter how difficult

Beginning the day with a promise to challenge negative ideas, suggestions and put-downs, and to walk away from the gloom and doom merchants, helps to reinforce positive thinking.

POSITIVE THINKING

TIPS

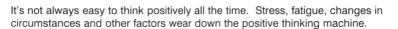

It's not always easy to think positively all the time. Stress, fatigue, changes in circumstances and other factors wear down the positive thinking machine.

Try to detach emotionally from a situation, be objective, see it from a different angle as a stranger might see it, and give yourself impartial advice.

Positive thinkers always have something to look forward to: 'When this is over I will ...'

Think big and be big. Think yes and it will be yes. Project positive thoughts to achieve positive action.

With a little practice every day, positive thinking will become second nature.

DISSATISFIED THINKING

WHAT IS IT?

Dissatisfied thinking is a characteristic of many people who feel that whatever they achieve in life isn't good enough.

Such people cite feeling:

- Empty (a hole which never fills up)
- As if something is missing (they need to keep achieving)
- Inferior to others
- That everything they have achieved (all their successes) is meaningless
- Discontented and unsettled

It has very little to do with wanting faster cars, better holidays or bigger houses, although some might try to fill the 'hole' with material possessions.

DISSATISFIED THINKING

CHARACTERISTICS

Dissatisfied thinkers:

- Feel tense all day   physically and mentally
- Experience a general anxiety and a fear that something bad is going to happen
- Compare themselves to others on a daily basis
- Live in the past or the future
- Don't trust, are suspicious and feel cheated
- Feel guilty if they get off the treadmill or don't live up to other people's expectations

They exhaust themselves because they can't stop the thoughts which echo: 'keep going... improve... perfect...'

DISSATISFIED THINKING

IN THE WORKPLACE

Here is an example of dissatisfied thinking at work:

The thought: Must stay later, come in earlier, do more, be seen

The reason: So busy, never enough time to complete the work

The motive: Being present will impress, lead to promotion

The fear: Will lose job to younger, brighter, more dynamic person

There is a **myth** that work is an on-going process and is never completed (like housework). Quantity can affect quality.

The **solution** to this is to remind dissatisfied thinkers repeatedly that quality has been achieved and that the working day is from 9 am to 5 pm and **not** longer.

DISSATISFIED THINKING

REASONS

Dissatisfied thinking is fuelled by:

- The need to keep up with other people
- Fear that if you relax and enjoy yourself something will happen to take it away
- An inner voice saying 'just a bit more, you're not there yet'
- Being told from an early age that 'great things are expected of you'
- Being unrealistic in your goals and personal ambitions
- Living by other people's values and not your own

DISSATISFIED THINKING

EXAMPLE

You dream of running a big company with a multi-million pound turnover. You have an MBA and excellent experience but are told that you lack the toughness required for such a role.

You are offered a post as Managing Director of a small thriving company which specialises in plastic components for the aircraft industry. The money and the perks are excellent but it isn't what you wanted. It isn't enough.

This type of negative thinking can be stopped by accepting your limitations, being proud of what you can do and making the most of your talents.

It is easy to miss out on good opportunities because you think they are not good enough.

DISSATISFIED THINKING

KNOW YOUR OWN MIND

Is your thinking driven by what others are doing?

Being over-aware of what others are doing puts pressure on dissatisfied thinkers who can never relax in case they are being judged:

- Sunday morning, lovely day; must mow the lawn (because Fred is doing his)
- New judo class has started in the area; seems as if all the kids in the neighbourhood are going, so must enrol mine (they already do trapeze, double bass, underwater cooking)
- The Thompsons are going to Kathmandu; forget Italy, we'd better look at Antarctica

With that mind-set, whatever you do will never be enough no matter what.

KNOW WHERE YOU STAND

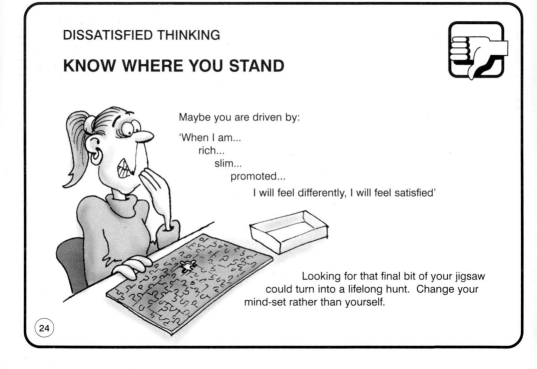

Maybe you are driven by:

'When I am...
rich...
slim...
promoted...

I will feel differently, I will feel satisfied'

Looking for that final bit of your jigsaw
could turn into a lifelong hunt. Change your
mind-set rather than yourself.

WANTS NOT NEEDS

Dissatisfied thinkers focus on what they **need** and not what they **want**:

> *'I need to go for promotion (money, status, keeping up) but want to stay where I am'*

> *'I want to give up the business but I need to prove I can keep going.'*

Make a checklist of your **needs** and **wants**. Are they the same? What drives **you**?
Spend more time thinking about what **you** really, really want!

DISSATISFIED THINKING

HOW TO CONQUER IT

We all experience dissatisfied thinking from time to time. How might it be conquered?

- Take a walk to the top of a steep hill, concentrating on your breathing and using all your senses; the sheer effort prevents you from thinking anything
- Think positive thoughts, focusing on what you have achieved
- Talk to someone who is satisfied with their life (there are many people with very few outward symbols of success who think 'This is enough')
- Use logical thinking to rationalise your thoughts
- Every day, tell yourself you're GREAT!

CREATIVE THINKING

HOW IT COMES ABOUT

Creative thinking skills are not taught. They do not require intelligence or even experience, although these qualities are needed to put creative ideas into practice.

Creative thinking is the result of right-brain activity - intuition, insight, inspiration - which is not readily encouraged in the education system. Indeed, such thought processes are often suppressed in favour of left-brain activities - logic, analysis and judgements.

'L' Logical brain   'R' aRtistic brain

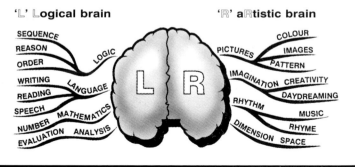

CREATIVE THINKING

BLOCKS TO CREATIVITY

Would-be creative thinkers mistakenly blame 'blocks' to their thought processes.
Here are some of them:

- Only clever, successful or artistic people can be creative
- You need to suffer hardship and pain to be truly creative (artist starving in the garret)
- Only young people have creative ideas
- Time, money and effort are needed; creative thinking is a luxury most of us can't afford
- It's only for men/women/the birds

Everyone has an Imagination which is the fuel for creative thinking. It is negative thinking which stops the creative process.

CREATIVE THINKING

TRIGGERING CREATIVE THOUGHTS

There are many ways to stimulate the flow of creative juices. Waiting for the Muse is too passive and a good excuse for not being inspired. So:

- Be hungry for information; read, read and read more

- Take up crafts and hobbies (you don't have to be good at them)

- Write, scribble, draw, design whatever comes into your head (often one idea leads to other better ideas)

- Brainstorm ideas with others

- Put yourself under reasonable pressure by setting goals and targets (caution: undue pressure leads to panic and stops the creative flow)

- Talk to children: often they make unusual associations between ideas (peanut butter and carrots, choc-ice and chips...)

CREATIVE THINKING

SELF-QUESTIONING

Talk to yourself! Ask yourself questions. Take on the role of the other person and debate with yourself

Ask the sort of questions that will help you to expand on an idea:

- What can I add or take away to change this?
- Could this be used for anything else?
- Could this be adapted - made smaller, bigger, different colour?
- Could I imitate without breaching copyright?
- Could several ideas be combined - all-purpose, multi purpose?
- Could I make it cheaper, simpler, more efficient, faster?

CREATIVE THINKING

EXERCISE

You've been offered a unique chance to take a six-month sabbatical. You want to spend the time creatively but don't quite know how. Try this exercise:

1. Take yourself off to somewhere peaceful with some blank sheets of paper and coloured pens
2. Jot down or draw different ideas as they come to you
3. Do this over a few days until you run out of ideas
4. Look for links between them
5. Take the most promising idea and develop it further
6. Now select one of these new ideas and expand on it
7. Repeat this exercise until your creative juices dry up

Stimulating creative thought processes needs some effort: 95% perspiration, 5% inspiration.

CREATIVE THINKING

EXAMPLES

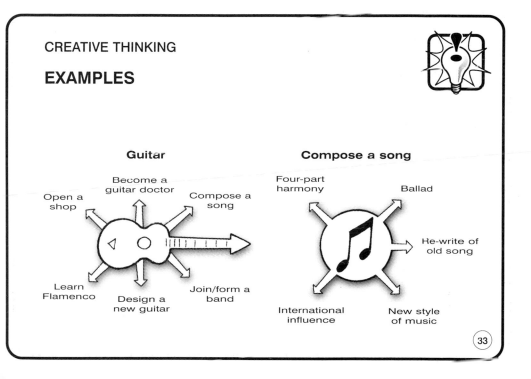

Guitar

Open a shop

Become a guitar doctor

Compose a song

Learn Flamenco

Design a new guitar

Join/form a band

Compose a song

Four-part harmony

Ballad

Re-write of old song

International influence

New style of music

CREATIVE THINKING

IN THE WORKPLACE

The most obvious uses of creative thinking are in product development, design and marketing. But, it can also be employed in other fields:

- Creating synergy between departments and people
- Managing time by combining complementary tasks
- Developing staff - multi-skilling and lateral job moves
- Developing systems - logic and creativity can work together
- Managing the direction of the business - vision, diversification, expansion

CREATING PEACE OF MIND

Creative thinking happens best when we are not trying. Being at peace with yourself and the world helps the imagination to function without interference.

Worrying about finding a solution to a problem is a sure way of not finding that solution. Worry is negative, unproductive and triggers one-track thinking. Try telling yourself that it doesn't matter if you don't come up with a good idea. Stop focusing too hard, then wait for the ideas to pop into your head (keep a notebook handy).

Don't confuse day-dreaming (passive and unrealistic) with creative thinking (active and realistic).

Read the chapter on bottom-line thinking if worry is getting in the way.

CREATIVE THINKING

HABIT STIFLES

There can be nothing more stifling to creative thinking than doing things through habit - casserole on Tuesdays, swimming on Sunday morning, meetings every Monday, sky-diving without a parachute on Saturday nights, etc.

Habits make us feel secure and take away the need to change. They also foster narrow-thinking and suspicion.

Examine your weekly/monthly pattern at home and work. Jot down activities you do through habit - same day, same approach. Select one or two for variation.

For example, take your staff on a walk instead of having a meeting and give them a problem to consider and discuss on the way (a lot more creative solutions will be found than sitting around the table watching the clock).

It's surprising how the smallest of changes can trigger creativity.

CREATIVE THINKING

TIPS

To harness your creative power:

- Find the ladder to climb the brick wall
- Avoid 'It's not for the likes of us' type people
- Practise clearing your mind for 20 minutes a day
- Keep an open mind - look at all viewpoints
- Always consider variations on an old theme
- Break old habits
- Never discard any ideas, no matter how irrational or impossible they seem

"Why doesn't he say something?"

"Don't disturb him. I think he's in one of his creative moods."

FINAL THOUGHT

For those of you who believe that creative thinking is a luxury you can't afford and you should really be spending your time on an MBA, remember what Albert Einstein said:

'Imagination is more important than knowledge'

LATERAL THINKING

LATERAL THINKING

OFF THE BEATEN TRACK

Lateral thinking is closely connected to creative thinking. It **generates** a wealth of ideas by pulling down the barriers defining a particular path. Lateral thinkers are prepared to wander into unknown territory rather than stick to an established route.

Lateral thinkers are like adventurous walkers. They don't follow the signposts which mark out a well-trodden route forward. Instead they cut new paths, leap ahead then backtrack, balance on a precipice or two and **eventually** reach their destination. Lateral thinking requires you to reach a conclusion but not necessarily in a logical, step by step manner.

LATERAL V LOGICAL THINKING

The key differences between lateral and logical thinkers are:

Lateral	Logical
• Wealth of ideas important	• How solid are they?
• Looks for least obvious answer	• Focuses on most obvious
• Seeks to challenge methods	• Sticks to proven methods
• Thought processes take sideways moves	• Moves vertically, step by step
• Looks for as many solutions as possible	• Uses judgement to select and reject ideas

Lateral thinkers are not born but made. This approach to thinking can be learned but needs to be practised regularly.

LATERAL THINKING

RE-SHAPING LONG-STANDING IDEAS

Lateral thinkers seek to challenge traditional approaches by dismantling the various elements and re-assembling them. For example:

The average worker puts in 40 hrs/week, typically between the hours of 9 am and 5 pm. The introduction of flexi-time challenged this by allowing individuals to choose their own start/finish times within agreed parameters.

Lateral thinking would take this further, suggesting that a significantly longer working day be introduced with a commensurate reduction in the overall number of working days in a year.

The logical thinker will present practical objections to this idea but the lateral thinker is not interested in the soundness of his proposals at this stage, only in the possibilities arising from challenging traditional thinking.

KEEPING AN OPEN MIND

Lateral thinkers **generate** new ideas without judging their merits. Compare, for example, the logical and lateral thinkers when asked to generate new ways of using a square silk scarf:

Logical	Lateral
• Headscarf/neckscarf	• The front part of a cushion cover
• Bandage	• Two dusters
• Sling	• A doll's dress
• Padding	• Part of a skirt
• Serviette	• Handkerchief
• Tray cloth	• A teddybear's hammock
• Tea towel	

Logical thinkers see the scarf as a) whole b) good quality c) something to be used purposefully.

Lateral thinkers see the scarf a) in several parts b) part of something else c) not something to be limited because it is silk.

IMPORTANCE OF NOT JUDGING

Tight schedules, pressurised lives, the 'need it by yesterday' approach to organisations drive us to think quickly, decide immediately, and then spend double the amount of time undoing the damage.

Ideas, however unlikely, need time to settle, germinate or die quietly. Lateral thinkers sleep on lumpy mattresses stuffed with unfinished, unconnected, undeveloped and even bizarre thoughts which they refuse to reject until the last possible moment.

LATERAL THINKING

USES

Lateral thinking can help you to:

1. Purposefully stimulate new ideas which can be developed creatively. Compare this to creative thinking which often relies on inspiration and is not necessarily structured.

2. Solve problems, requiring insight and a re-shaping of existing approaches.

3. Develop and improve designs.

4. Keep an open mind. The lateral thinker is consciously aware that things might not be what they seem. This does not mean constantly questioning or denying everything: 'Well, you say it's raining. But is this what we would define as rain?'

LATERAL THINKING

HOW TO ENCOURAGE IT

If lateral thinking is about rearranging information and looking at different ways of doing things, then there are several ways in which this can be constructively encouraged:

1. By reversing situations

For example, students instruct teachers, customers help shop assistants, alimony is fixed before marriage. It doesn't matter how ridiculous the idea is; you don't know where it might lead.

2. By removing the dominant feature within an idea

For example, money might be the dominant obstacle to developing a new product. Remove the need for money and continue the discussions without allowing money to be mentioned. A way round the problem might emerge once the problem no longer blocks the thought processes.

FORMAL BRAINSTORMING

Brainstorming to encourage lateral thinking should be:

- Within a formal setting
- Of a fixed time limit
- Organised in its approach
- Include a chairperson and note-taker
- Exclude evaluation during the session
- Incorporate a degree of structure, ie: as much free thinking as possible, but about the topic only

STOP THIEF!

Why is a lateral thinker like a burglar?

Sneaking in through a side gate (although he planned to enter via the back of the property) a burglar breaks a window and enters the house with the intention of stealing a camcorder kept in the study. However, he spots a diamond ring and necklace on the kitchen worktop. He forgets all about the camcorder and makes off with the jewellery.

The lateral thinker can choose not to approach the problem by the most obvious and planned route (like the burglar) in the hope of stumbling across something which was not being sought in the first place.

LATERAL THINKING

CHALLENGING ASSUMPTIONS

A computer engineer received a call from a client complaining that his printer wasn't working. Between them they went through all the possibilities and options on the telephone but without success. So, the engineer arranged to visit the client to repair the printer. A few minutes before setting off, she called the client again:

'Have you switched on the printer?'

'What do you think I am?'

' Please would you double check?'

Silence.

' Somebody unplugged it. Don't understand why. I just assumed....'

' Thanks. That's saved me a journey.'

While lateral thinkers don't settle for the obvious, they never overlook it or make assumptions.

LATERAL THINKING

TIPS

Here are some tips for putting lateral thinking into practice:

1. Invest in Edward de Bono's books, 'Lateral Thinking' and 'The Five Day Thinking Course'.

2. Think up as many ideas as possible for solving a problem. Don't judge any of them as being ridiculous; the earth being round was considered a crazy idea, as was going to the moon!

3. Think from the opposite, upside down, inside out, round about. Look for the least obvious start points, even if there is a brick wall against them.

4. Practise lateral thinking even when you know there is only one solution. (But do you?)

LOGICAL THINKING

LOGICAL THINKING

A SAFE PROCESS

According to popular misconception, logical thinking is often attributed to the normal functioning of the male brain. In fact, we **all** have the skill to adopt an unemotional, detached, step-by-step approach to our thinking processes.

Logical thinking is **safe** as there is no room for untested ideas which pop into our heads at random. This important feature makes it an essential component of the thinker's portfolio.

However, it is easy to rely too heavily on logic. We need to know when to switch it off and make room for more creative and imaginative ideas.

WHO'S GOOD AT IT?

A good logical thinker is someone who:

- Is well organised
- Pays attention to the smallest detail
- Concentrates on fact and not fantasy
- Can work within a rigid framework
- Does not allow personal feelings to colour judgement
- Stays detached
- Has lots of patience to eliminate variables through reasoning
- Has no sudden urge to leap into unknown territory!

If you don't immediately identify with these traits, don't despair.
You can still develop sound logical thinking skills.

RIGHT, BUT PREFERABLE?

More importantly, logical thinking requires the **acceptance** of the conclusion even if it is not something we want it to be. For example, it is logical that:

We spend a £2,000 windfall paying off the credit card rather than on two nights in Las Vegas. (Because it reduces debt, gets rid of the interest, puts us in a stronger financial position, etc.) The fact that it is no fun and is not what we really want to do is immaterial.

- What would the creative thinker do?
- How would the positive thinker see it?
- How might a flash of intuition influence the decision?

CHALLENGING & PURPOSEFUL

Logical thinking means using information for a particular purpose and not for the sake of it. Consequently, it provides a focus and a clear direction whilst disciplining, stretching and challenging the mind.

It can be particularly satisfying to take apart the main components of a problem or decision and, by adopting a logical approach, analyse each one in order to find a solution.

OBJECTIVITY

A logical approach to situations will also eliminate bias and opinion and will ensure fairness.

To fully understand a problem, it is necessary to take it apart and break it down into its various components for careful analysis.

Business decisions rely heavily on this process. A small company which runs into financial difficulties will need to analyse very carefully its strengths, current weaknesses, opportunities and threats (SWOT) before re-shaping its finances. One false move could mean disaster.

A STEP-BY-STEP APPROACH

A company director wishing to introduce a new product range will need to examine carefully all the issues involved. This means asking questions:

Who? What? Where? When? How?

By taking a step-by-step approach, testing possible links, considering all possible consequences, there is a strong probability that disasters will be avoided.

Whilst creative, lateral and even intuitive thinking might have a place in generating new business ideas, it is the sound, relatively safe, process of logical thinking which dominates business life.

TIPS

Logical thinking is like climbing a tree.
This is how to go about it:

1. Be sure why you want to climb the tree (to explore is not a good enough reason for the logical thinker).

2. Make sure you have the right equipment (ie: the means to reach your goal, such as information).

3. Choose the most obvious route (where the branches appear strongest).

4. Get a firm footing at each stage before moving on. Keep looking ahead.

TIPS (Cont'd)

5. Ignore the branches with the juicy fruit if they are not on your route!

6. Make sure each step has a purpose and that it is the right step to take.

7. Once you have reached the top (your goal) that is the end of the exercise.

Compare this approach with that of the creative thinker, who might try to play Tarzan, or the positive thinker, who believes there is more tree to climb and will argue that you just can't see it yet!

DRAWBACKS

If logical thinking is safe, fair and, according to many, the only way to think, then why read the other chapters in this book?

Logical thinking has its drawbacks:

- It is inflexible and therefore prevents creativity
- It requires paying attention to detail which can be laborious for some
- Used all the time, it would indicate a lack of self-confidence and initiative
- It can sometimes over-ride other thought processes and lead to missed opportunities
- It can be time-consuming

Whatever your views on logical thinking, it should complement your wide range of thinking skills.

BOTTOM-LINE THINKING

PROVIDING REASSURANCE

Making a decision or taking a risk is not something all of us do easily. We may soul search for weeks, even months, and still not reach a conclusion or take any action.

This is often because we fear the consequences when we take a leap into the unknown.

Living in today's uncertain if not chaotic times means we are having to make changes in our work, homes and lifestyles whether we like it or not.

Bottom-line thinking can provide the reassurance we need to move on.

BOTTOM-LINE THINKING

AID TO DECISION-MAKING

Bottom-line thinking involves collecting as much information as possible and making a **realistic** assessment of the worst possible scenario (WPS).

Sit down alone and, without being distracted, jot down **all** the possible consequences of the decision you have to make. Now draw a red ring around the one you fear most. (Ignore the hot sweats and the urge to be sick.)

Take a separate piece of paper and in big black letters write it down again. Look at it hard. Imagine it has happened. If you can accept it, the decision is easy. If not, ask yourself 'Why not?'.

EXAMPLE

Here's an example of how bottom-line thinking works in practice:

Joe's firm had asked for voluntary redundancies for the second time. Joe was sure that if he didn't put his name forward it would only be a matter of time before he was required to leave. The firm had offered a year's salary and good references. Joe's head was reeling from indecision until he applied some bottom-line thinking.

EXAMPLE (Cont'd)

Joe decided that the absolute bottom-line for him was not being able to get any sort of job again. He imagined himself in that situation and began to think of a lifestyle which did not require him to work in a conventional sense (eg: charity work overseas, voluntary work in hospitals, beachcomber, self-employment, a monastery).

Suddenly he felt liberated. The fear drained away. A world of possibilities opened up as a result of his bottom-line thinking, once he had stared the WPS in the face and accepted it.

BOTTOM-LINE THINKING

EXERCISE

Isolate a decision you have to make or a situation which is worrying you. It may be something as simple as joining a keep-fit club, where you don't know anyone, or it may entail a major life-change.

Choose a sunny day and go off to the park. Sit under a shady tree, watch the children playing and spend 10 minutes doing this exercise:

Study your WPS. How do you feel? Imagine it has happened. Now look around you: do you see colour, feel the sun, hear laughter?

Look again at your WPS. Is that really the worst thing that could happen to you?

BENEFITS

Bottom-line thinking gives us:

- A concrete (rather than imaginary) view of the worst possible outcome to a situation
- A better grip on our fear
- A chance to put things into perspective and see beyond our personal anxiety
- Control over our next move
- An appreciation of what is really important to us
- A more open mind to alternatives and solutions

BOTTOM-LINE THINKING

STRIPPING AWAY THE LAYERS

From time to time we all feel a vague sense of unease. Outside stresses, endless changes, bad news and general fatigue can result in nagging doubts about our abilities, future prospects and choices.

While bottom-line thinking can be applied to decision-making and problem-solving, it can also be used to soul search - to strip away the layers and find out what we really want rather than what we think we should want.

BOTTOM-LINE THINKING

STRIPPING AWAY THE LAYERS
CASE STUDY

Tom had followed his father into the family law firm. At 05 he had a mild heart attack. During that time he was able to review his life and imagined himself following his dream of setting up a windsurfing school in Cyprus. He collected lots of information, drew up a business plan and then thought through the WPS should it not be successful.

Tom's bottom-line thinking stripped away the quest for material things (status, high income, big home, BMW) until he reached the bottom layer - health, well-being, contentment (none of which he had at that moment).

Tom accepted that he might lose his 'things' in exchange for the chance of a longer, more rewarding, life. Without some bottom-line thinking, Tom would have carried on as before.

BOTTOM-LINE THINKING

WHEN TO USE IT

- When making a decision
- If you are anxious about a decision already made
- When wanting to make a change
- If you are feeling dissatisfied or restless
- When faced with a threat or challenge
- When you want to say NO

Bottom-line thinking makes you:

- Face the facts
- Accept that the WPS could in the long-run be the best thing that happened to you
- Realise that once you are on the bottom the only way is **up**!

OVER-THINKING &
NON-THINKING

OVER-THINKING

HOW IT OCCURS

Over-thinking happens when the mind latches on to a particular thought, often negative, and exaggerates its importance. It looms large and menacing and can lead to a total preoccupation or even obsession.

Thinking through problems is healthy and stimulating but when the process becomes confused and turbulent it can have a detrimental effect on progress and even on health.

Over-thinking occurs through:

- Misunderstandings
- Not listening or accepting true explanations
- As a result of being tired, unwell or stressed
- Fear, anger or other strong emotions
- By reading too much into a situation

OVER-THINKING

WHO IS AT RISK?

The people most at risk of over-thinking are those who:

- Spend too much time alone
- Haven't enough to stimulate them or keep them interested
- Are looking for a fight/someone to blame
- Can't find a rational explanation for something that's happened
- Can't switch off and relax
- Are used to analysing things in great detail and can't accept things at face value

OVER-THINKING

EXAMPLE

Often it is irrelevant or insignificant information which goes round and round in the head, creating impasses in the rational thought process.

Take the case of Samantha Smith who took up a new post with an engineering company. She was a competent bilingual secretary and was looking forward to using her German.

Her line manager was warm and friendly at first until Samantha was asked to accompany the Sales Director to Germany. When Samantha returned she felt she couldn't do anything right. Her manager seemed to be cold and aloof towards her and Samantha found herself working later and later into the evening. She became convinced that there was a conspiracy to make life so uncomfortable that she would have to leave.

A month later everyone in the department - herself included - was given a huge bonus as a thank you for their hard work in securing a major contract in Frankfurt. Her fears were totally unfounded.

OVER-THINKING

CONSEQUENCES

Over-thinking can become addictive. It can also lead to a number of problems:

- False accusations made against people at work, at home and among friends
- Heightened awareness of what's going on around
- Unnecessary anxiety
- Too much energy and focus in trying to find proof to justify such thoughts
- A closed mind
- Loss of interest in anything other than the pre-occupation

OVER-THINKING

HOW TO STOP

One of the main problems is recognising that there is a problem!

If someone you know is behaving like a 'dog with a bone' over a particular issue and it seems to be going on and on, there are several ways you can help:

- Suggest the person takes a long break and goes walking, sailing, travelling (this will help focus the mind on something else)

- If the over-thinking is as a result of fear (eg: job loss) help with some bottom-line thinking

- Get other people involved and encourage the person to socialise, but ban the dreaded topic of discussion for the evening

- Suggest relaxation programmes

ABSORB, NOT PROCESS

If the brain really is like a computer we should be able to switch it off and pull out the plug. Easier said than done.

We need to get into a **non-thinking** state from time to time by allowing information to be absorbed through the senses but not processed (eg: watching the tide without thinking about the whys and wherefores of it).

The non-thinking state is not total shut-down (that would be the comatose state). It is about taking in what we see and hear at face value and enjoying it for its own sake. In our non-thinking state we don't analyse, crystallise, summarise or fantasise.

BENEFITS

- Gives the brain a holiday
- Gives ourselves some breathing space
- Resolves over-thinking
- Helps us to just **be** rather than **do**
- Induces relaxation

Doesn't sleep have the same effect?
Dreams and nightmares result from
the brain unravelling the day's events.
The non-thinking state simply asks
you to do nothing that requires
any thinking at all.

TIPS

The non-thinking state can be achieved through:

- Repetitive physical activity - digging, pumping iron, running, etc (you become more conscious of your breathing, sweating and heart pumping and less aware of your thoughts)

- Meditation: chant a mantra (TM) for 20 minutes and clear your head of clutter (I'd need a skip to take mine away, I hear you say!)

- Deep relaxation: there are tapes, books and classes designed to help you reach such a state

- Letting your mind go a complete blank: stare into space, let your body go limp, push out any thought - pleasurable or not - as it enters your head (with practice it becomes easier and, once again, there are self-help books available)

NON-THINKING

HOW NOT TO ACHIEVE IT

- By trying to force it: if the non-thinking state is difficult to achieve at first, give up and try later

- By sitting in a room full of stimuli: quiet and bland surroundings help achieve the best results

- By feeling physically uncomfortable before you start: there's nothing worse than trying to block out your thoughts when you are desperate for the loo

- By over-eating and over-drinking

INTUITIVE THINKING & MAGICAL THINKING

A PLACE FOR IT?

'Intuition - immediate apprehension by the mind without reasoning: immediate insight' (Oxford dictionary definition).

The use of intuition in problem-solving, decision-making and business and product development would be considered by most to be irrational, illogical, dangerous and even downright crazy.

That's because it is not fully understood. Besides, it is usually women who are given the dubious credit for being intuitive.

Yet, don't we **all** have gut feelings, hunches about things or, without knowing why, just sense that something is right (or wrong)?

CASE STUDY

You're interviewing a candidate for a job in your department. She meets all the requirements - experience, qualifications, personal qualities, attitude and an ability to work in a team - and appears to be the 'ideal' candidate.

However, you have a strange feeling that she is going to cause trouble for the firm. You have no evidence and your colleagues think you've been overworking when you try to argue your case. Yet the sense of knowing her selection would be a bad decision almost overwhelms you.

Six months later the same person embezzles company funds and runs off with important customer information. You didn't listen and trust your intuitive mind.

Happily, it works in reverse. Look around your department. Is there someone you took a risk with because your gut instinct told you to?

INTUITIVE THINKING

A THIRD DIMENSION

Intuitive thinking is a must for your portfolio of thinking skills. It provides a third dimension to how you view situations and people. You can get a tremor of excitement when your intuitive thoughts are right.

Consider for a moment how much intuitive thinking you do, at a basic level, on a day-to-day basis.

Examples

- You read a draft of a new marketing leaflet and it 'doesn't sound quite right'; you can't put your finger on why

- You examine a prototype of a new product and although the pieces are in the right place, it 'doesn't look right'

- A client doesn't 'sound quite right' on the phone

- 'I've just had a brainwave; don't laugh, but I think it's brilliant'

WHEN TO ACT ON INTUITION

Intuition can be the brain's way of telling you to be careful - to investigate a bit further before making a commitment. It can over-ride all other sorts of thinking processes, almost as a safety-switch.

Use intuition in this way:

1. Listen to what it is telling you. If it makes you feel uncomfortable (some people become hot and agitated when their intuitive mind is screaming at them) then ...

2. Share it with a close friend or colleague. See if they have the same views.

3. Use other sorts of thinking (logical, for example) to block it out. If it refuses to go away and you don't follow it, then ...

4. Build in a contingency plan in case your intuition is right and you are wrong!

NOT ONLY INSTINCT

Intuitive thinking is not just about instincts, premonitions and flashes of insight.

We **all** get strange thoughts from time to time and in some cases there is a pattern to them. However, it is unlikely that we would ever consider analysing them, preferring to put such thoughts down to an over-active mind.

THIRD 'EYE'

A doctor who was very successful and happy in his work repeatedly had strange thoughts about a lawnmower. He decided it was guilt over not doing the garden. The thoughts persisted: vivid, colourful, detailed and they began to scream at him. He went to see his friend who was a psychiatrist. One evening he drew the lawnmower just as he saw it in his mind's eye and realised it was a gadget of the future. Other thoughts began to jostle for room - a big house, beach, private plane, himself with the Mayor of Florida. Against all common sense he developed a prototype of the lawnmower, sold it to a big American company and........ You can guess the rest.

Was it a coincidence? Why a lawnmower? Why him?

We can't always answer these questions but we should be aware when our third eye is roving into the future on our behalf.

INTUITIVE THINKING

TIPS

Here are some tips to develop your intuitive thinking skills:

- Switch your mind off; don't think, just **feel** and **sense**
- Relax
- Record everything that comes into your mind - don't analyse it
- Don't dismiss or judge anything
- Try to recall dreams as soon as you wake
- Record how you feel about these intuitive thoughts and dreams

Repeat the process over a period of three months and see if there is a pattern. Is the small voice in your head trying to tell you something?

FACT OR FICTION?

- 'It came to me as if by magic!'
- 'This photocopier must be jinxed.'

Two examples of how 'magical' thoughts invade our minds, often because there is no other possible explanation for what is happening.

Magical thinking might be described as **lucky thinking**.

How many times have you been told to think lucky and you'll be lucky? Does it work? In my experience, often it does.

MAGICAL THINKING

BEHAVIOURAL LINKS

There is a close link between behaviour and lucky or unlucky thought processes:

- We see 4-leaf clover, black cats and horseshoes as good luck
- We touch wood, throw salt over our shoulder and walk round ladders to avoid bad luck
- We wear that particular shirt or blouse that always brings us good luck

Don't discard these beliefs as childish nonsense. Who knows, they could work magic for you!